SPIRITUAL ECOLOGY

10 Practices to Reawaken the Sacred in Everyday Life

LLEWELLYN VAUGHAN-LEE *and* HILARY HART

THE GOLDEN SUFI CENTER

SPIRITUAL ECOLOGY

*10 Practices to Reawaken
the Sacred in Everyday Life*

**LLEWELLYN VAUGHAN-LEE
and HILARY HART**

First published in the United States in 2017 by
The Golden Sufi Center
P.O. Box 456, Point Reyes, California 94956
www.goldensufi.org

ISBN: 978-1-941394-18-2

Printed and bound in the USA.

Library of Congress Cataloging-in-Publication Data
Names: Vaughan-Lee, Llewellyn, author. | Hart, Hilary, 1963- author.
Title: Spiritual ecology : 10 practices to reawaken the sacred in
everyday life / by Llewellyn Vaughan-Lee and Hilary Hart.
Description: Point Reyes, California : Golden Sufi Center, [2017] |
  Includes bibliographical references.
Identifiers: LCCN 2016049843 (print) | LCCN 2017000637 (ebook) |
  ISBN 9781941394182 (pbk. : alk. paper) | ISBN 9781941394199 (PDF) |
  ISBN 9781941394205 (ePub) | ISBN 9781941394212 (Mobi (Kindle))
Subjects: LCSH: Human ecology--Religious aspects. |
  Environmentalism--Religious aspects.
Classification: LCC GF80 .V39 2017 (print) | LCC GF80 (ebook) | DDC
  201/.77--dc23
LC record available at https://lccn.loc.gov/2016049843

CONTENTS

Introduction   i

1. Walking   1

2. Breathing   9

3. Gardening   19

4. Seeds and Their Stories   27

5. Cooking with Love   37

6. Cleaning   47

7. Simplicity   57

8. Prayer   67

9. Death   77

10. Meaning and the Sacred   87

Notes   92
Acknowledgments   96

The seeds of joy are everywhere in life.

INTRODUCTION

SPIRITUAL ECOLOGY arises out of the need for a spiritual response to our present ecological crisis. Without including a spiritual dimension to our response to "the cry of the Earth," we are in danger of reconstellating the same materialistic paradigm that has created our present consumer-driven ecocide. Our book *Spiritual Ecology: The Cry of the Earth* grew out of this need. After reading the urgent call articulated there by spiritual teachers, scientists, and indigenous leaders from many different traditions to regain a connection to the sacred, many people, especially young people, responded, "What should I do?" This small book, *Spiritual Ecology: 10 Practices to Reawaken the Sacred in Everyday Life,* suggests a number of simple spiritual practices aimed at restoring our connection to the sacred in everyday life.

When I arrived at my teacher's doorstep, I was nineteen and battered from living in a soulless, materialistic world, one without any recognition of the sacred, especially the sacred within creation. The first practice that she gave me was "The Practice of the Presence of God," as described by Brother Lawrence, a seventeenth-century Carmelite lay monk. He had been a soldier and adventurer and was not allowed to be ordained as monk, but he worked in the monastery, often in the kitchens. He developed a simple and powerful practice of the awareness of the Divine in everyday activities. He washed the potatoes with God, chopped the carrots with God, performed every activity of his day with God, until the presence of God became indwelling in every aspect of his life. In many ways this practice that celebrates the Divine, the sacred, within all of our activities is all one needs to awaken to the sacred nature of creation.[1]

I had learned to meditate when I was sixteen, but this was the first spiritual practice that oriented me towards the outer world, towards an experience of the sacred within the physical world around me and under my feet. Through it I learned that in the outer world of forms, through the experience of the senses, we can come to experience and know the Divine that is within everything that exists. We can come closer to the real mystery of creation, what the Sufis call "the secret of the word *'Kun!'* ('Be!')."[2]

So when I was sitting, and walking, with that question about spiritual ecology—"What should I do?"—I understood that we need first to return to, and reconnect with, the sacred nature of creation. Only from the foundation of this lived relationship can we attempt to bring the world back into balance, heal and redeem what our present culture has destroyed and desecrated with its greed and soulless materialism. Our outer actions need to be based upon this inner connection. I also realized that over the years since I first arrived on my teacher's doorstep and started practicing the presence of God, I had developed certain practices that have helped me with this work. And Hilary Hart has kindly written exercises that follow each text, to help the reader more fully engage with these practices.

Within these ten practices, I have not included what is in many ways the simplest and most obvious, and for many people the most healing—spending time in nature. Walking, sitting, and being in nature are direct ways to reconnect with beauty, wonder, and a sense of the sacred. Being in the wind without a coat, really looking at the moon and seeing stars, listening to water in a stream, just being in a city park filled with trees or flowers, we are drawn out of ourselves. We feel what today's culture so easily obscures, and by reflection we are drawn back to our essential sacred nature, a sacred land. But what I am attempting to share with these practices is that "nature" is not limited to a landscape or place, but is around and within us all of the time. We do not need to "travel" to find this connection—in a car, by bike or train—but can allow it to come alive in our ordinary life, with every breath, with every step. The sacred is not a place to *go*, but a *state of being*.

These are simple practices of returning to the sacred in everyday life. They are not specifically Sufi practices, though they have been influenced by the love and awareness that are part of the Sufi path. I hope that the reader finds them helpful—stepping stones to reconnect with the sacred foundation of all life.

Walk as if you are kissing the Earth with your feet.

Thich Nhat Hanh

1. WALKING

I have always loved to walk early in the morning, to sense the Earth at the beginning of a day, to feel Her pulse, Her beauty and magic, before thoughts and demands clutter my day. Waking early, I have a hot cup of tea, meditate in silence, and then, as soon as the first light comes, I walk down the hill to the road beside the wetlands where I live. Sometimes the frost is sparkling around me, sometimes the water is clouded with fog, an egret appearing white against the reeds. This is another time of silent meditation, walking, breathing, feeling the Earth. I try to be as empty as possible, just to be present in the half-light, aware of what is around me. Prayer, meditation, presence, awareness—these are just words for a practice that immerses me in a mystery we call nature. Here the sacred speaks to me in its own language, and I try to listen.

Now I live beside the wetlands, and the tidal water is part of this meeting, this communion. Other times, in other landscapes, it has been rivers and streams, the sounds of waterfowls' wings, the dawn rising across meadows. Or in forests, a different bird chorus, animals skittering across the path, a deer and her young. Always it is a listening awareness, a deep receptivity to what is around me, an honoring of a world other than people. It is a remembrance of what is essential, elemental, and its nourishment carries me through the day. It is a return to the sacred, sensed and felt, without words or thoughts—a primal consciousness as if of the first day.

This is a practice that has been with me since my teens—when I first started to meditate I also needed to walk. It was not taught or learned, but came as a need, a way to be, an antidote to much of the world around me—a world of people and problems, demands and desires. When one foot follows the other and the day has hardly begun, it seems these demands cannot touch me, as if I am immersed in something simpler, more essential. Placing each foot on the earth is a practice, but a practice that comes from my own roots, not a book or a teacher. Later I came to hear it called "walking in a sacred manner," and it is sacred, a return to what is sacred. But it also is deeper or more primal than any purpose. Nature speaks to me and I listen. Nature calls and something deep within me responds, and I just need to give it space. I am part of a life far greater than any "me."

The Earth gives us sustenance: the air we breathe, the food we eat. She is generous in so many ways, even as we forget Her and abuse Her. But there is also this deeper nourishment, this invisible, intangible giving. My early morning walk is a communion—if I am receptive, it is a wine drunk deeply. It comes through Her landscape, moss dripping from the trees, white and pink blossoms welcoming spring, the cry of a sea bird. Those first rays of sunrise are always a blessing. I do not understand this with my mind, but my soul feels it, needs it. Once again we are back at the beginning, in that elemental world we never truly leave. Our present culture may have forgotten it, disowned it, covered it over, may pretend we no longer need this communion, but my soul and my feet know otherwise. This is the landscape of the soul as much as it is the wetlands stretching towards the ocean. But it is also any landscape we walk. A walk on city streets is made of the same elements: feet touching ground, the rhythm of walking, breathing, the same sky overhead, the wind touching the face.

I would like to say it is easy, but so often I have to remember to reconnect, to empty the clutter of the coming day from my mind, my everyday thoughts. I have to stay in a place of awareness, sense my feet, feel the air, listen. I have to remember that I am not separate but part of everything around me. I have to push aside this great myth of separation, the great untruth. We are the air we breathe, the earth we touch, the same one life, alive in so many ways. We are the Earth awakening in the early morning, just as we are the buds breaking into color in the spring. To be fully alive is to feel how we are part of this embracing mystery. My morning walk is a remembrance, a reconnection, experienced in the body and felt in the soul.

WALKING PRACTICE

Walking reinforces our connection to the Earth, one step at a time. Attuning to the rhythms of one's feet, the swaying of one's arms, the in and out of breath, the ways walking moves us through time and space, helps develop this relationship, reminding us consciously and unconsciously just how much a part of nature we are. Nature is cyclic and rhythmic, and walking—when we are not focused on where we are going—attunes us to this non-linear reality.

Walking practice is perhaps best begun alone, when the intimacy of nature's communication can be sensed without distraction. Just as when we meet a lover in the early part of a relationship, we do not want to share that meeting with others. Choose a time when you can be alone, when listening, hearing, and sensing can take place. Perhaps the start or the end of the day, before life's clamoring takes hold or after it lets go. Lunchtime or an afternoon break from work might be more difficult, but if that is the time available, then make sure the walk is long enough for you to let go of work thoughts or tensions of the day.

Turn off the cell phone, or better yet, leave it at home or the office. There is a way that the vulnerabilities that come with being alive have been squelched by our daily-life safety tools, like cell phones. If you can be without the protection and constant access they provide, try it. Social media will not miss documentation from your walk.

🌿 *Find a park or a path* through a quiet woods if you can. Let the rhythm of your steps soothe your mind and create a space for listening. Feel how your feet connect with the earth, how the air moves through your lungs. Follow your attention as it is drawn inward and outward both—to the inner movements of your body and to the feeling of warmth or cold, the sight of birds, the sound of a distant plane. Let your thoughts and impressions move through and out, as part of the natural rhythm of walking. Just as we come back to the breath in silent meditation, return your attention to your feet and their meeting and letting go of the ground.

🌿 *Commit to walking every day* if you can. Walk without expectation, with an attitude of openness and gratitude. If you feel a longing inside you—a need to connect, a desire to be closer to nature—let it motivate and guide you.

The nineteenth-century existential philosopher Søren Kierkegaard once wrote in a letter to his niece, "Every day, I walk myself into a state of well-being and walk away from every illness. I have walked myself into my best thoughts, and I know of no thought so burdensome that one cannot walk away from it."

*Breathe slowly, silently, and naturally. When you inhale
through the nose, the belly gently expands. When you exhale
through the mouth, it releases, effortlessly.*

*With each inhalation imagine
that you are drawing-in the pure energy of the universe.
It spreads through your entire body, refreshing
and renewing you. With each exhalation, you
release the old, unneeded energy.*

Taoist breathing practice[3]

2. BREATHING

Breathing is living. If we are not breathing we are not alive. Breathing is the most primal rhythm of our life, along with the beating of the heart. With every breath we bring the oxygen we need into our blood and body. But how many of us breathe consciously, are aware of the breath?

My teacher had been trained in India, and she taught me a yogic breath: when you breathe in you feel your belly expand, when you breathe out you feel it come back in. This is a way of breathing deeply, with awareness, very different from the shallow breathing of those who are so busy with their lives they are barely aware of their breath at all, who have forgotten how to breathe deeply or—because they are so disconnected—how to live deeply. Ever since then I always breathe in the way my teacher taught me. It is a profoundly purifying practice, and like all true practices, what begins with effort and attention eventually becomes just a way of life, a natural way to breathe. My teacher's teacher was trained in the old ways, and when he meditated there was no in- or out-breath; he breathed "internally" so as not to disturb his meditation. Such yogic techniques are far beyond me, but simple awareness of breath, belly expanding and contracting, is central to my life. It is so simple, yet it is so profound.

The breath is central to spiritual practices across most of the spiritual traditions.[4] Yogis practice *pranayama*, the control of the breath; Taoists use breath control to increase their *chi*, their life force. Vipassana meditation begins with focusing attention on the breath in order to concentrate and clear the mind. Sufi *dhikrs* are chanted or repeated with the breath, and the Jesus Prayer practiced in the Orthodox Church is also said in conjunction with the breath. My own Naqshbandi Sufi tradition teaches that awareness of breath is the foundation of inner work: "The more one is able to be conscious of one's breathing, the stronger is one's inner life."[5]

The soul has also long been thought to be in the breath and is sometimes visualized as a breath body. In Sufi teachings the soul comes into the body with every out-breath, and with each in-breath returns to its spiritual dimension. This is why the last breath of a dying person is said to be an in-breath, their last gasp of air. On that final in-breath the soul returns to its own plane and does not come back into the body.[6] While we are alive, with each cycle of the breath the soul makes its journey into this world and then back to the Source. Spiritually we aspire to make this journey conscious.

It is the lived prayer of the soul, an offering of our self to the mystery of life and its all-embracing relationship to the Divine. With each breath we consciously connect the two worlds, the world of the spirit and the physical world. We are present in the love affair that is the relationship between the Creator and the creation.

But we no longer recognize that connection of love between the worlds, between spirit and matter. Our world is starving for spiritual nourishment as we collectively assert that the material world is all that exists. Our consciousness then creates a barrier between the worlds, rather than helping to link inner and outer: isolating the world soul (the spiritual principle within matter) from the manifest world, we choke the flow of spirit into matter, and the conscious connection of the soul to the outer world is lost. In the process, the world soul, the *anima mundi*, also becomes increasingly disconnected from the outer world.

Breath connects matter and spirit. This is the basis of the simple Tibetan healing practice of visualizing the breath in the part of the body that needs healing: *prana*, life force, follows the breath, and, flowing from the inner to outer world, brings energy and healing to where it is directed.[7] If we are conscious of our breath in our daily life, we connect the two worlds and bring a healing energy from the inner into the outer. When we breathe consciously, we live the cycle of creation, both for ourself and for the world. We help to reconnect the world and its soul.

Returning to the breath is a return to the soul, a re-connection with what is sacred. This simple and primary practice is essential for well-being and for healing, for the individual and the whole. When I walk I like to be aware of the breath, of my feet touching the ground in harmony with the rhythm of the breath. As that rhythm starts to take over, inner and outer once again start to flow together, and then the soul can start to sing, to sing the wonder of creation, the love song of all of life. I can feel it in the air around, in the magic present in nature.

In our present culture we have forgotten so much. We have forgotten the song of creation, the love song of the world soul. And we have forgotten how to breathe. We no longer connect the worlds together. We no longer live the mystery of the sacred. And so we are starved, isolated in a disconnected world, seeking distraction after distraction. But within us we have the simple tools of reconnection. Breath is our most primary prayer, just as it is a primary source of life. And it carries the secret of our connection to the sacred.

Remember to breathe and you remember what it means to be alive. Follow the breath and you follow the secret rhythm of life. Improving your breath you improve the flow of energy, of *chi*. Breathing well is vitally impor-tant for your health—the deeper the breath, the more you are able to dissolve energy blockages in your mind/body. This is well-known. But we are not separate; everything is interconnected. Our breathing is also linked to the energy flow of creation. When we breathe well we affect not just our own body but also the body of the whole; connecting with our soul, we connect with the world soul. We bring a healing energy into life itself and help awaken the sacred within creation.

Spiritual ecology is a recognition of the need to return to the source of our own sacred nature, and of the spiritual practices that affect both the individual and the whole, practices that can, through our own individual awareness and action, also help restore the connection between the Earth and its own Source. With the simple practice of awareness of breath we can help to keep this connection alive. We can help the pure energy of life flow between the worlds.

BREATHING PRACTICE

Because you are always breathing, you always have access to the sacred; you always have a refuge in the Real. This understanding informs a breathing practice that is simple, available, and easeful. You do not need to search for your breath or force yourself to breathe. This practice is about shifting your attention to what is already happening, already sustaining you.

❦ *Wherever you are,* whatever you are doing, you can pay attention to your breath. Listen to your breath, feel your breath, be aware of your breath. Sensing how the breath infuses the body, you attune to a tenderness and a quietness within life. In today's over-stimulated world, most of us need access to this refuge that is gentle and rhythmic, simple and alive.

❦ *Bring your attention to your breath* throughout the day—when you are standing in a grocery line, waiting for a meeting to begin, watching a movie, or on hold with technical support. If you have a meditation practice, you might choose to begin meditation by following your breath as a means of relaxing into your body. At night, lying in bed, you can feel the weight of your body rise and sink gently before you go to sleep.

🍃 *Notice the state of your body as you breathe.* It can happen that as you put your attention on your breath, your breath can quicken and your body can contract because you are suddenly more conscious than you have been, more awake or self-conscious. In the West, we are used to being highly stressed and stimulated, and our sensitive nervous systems can overreact to even the simplest switching-on of attention. In such a case, start a breathing practice combined with a walking practice, which naturally relaxes the body and mind. Or, consciously extend your belly outward as you inhale, and contract as you exhale. Using your muscles in this way can release some tension, and after a few such breaths, you can return to a more relaxed breathing.

🍃 *See if you can feel your breath* reaching beyond the familiar boundaries of your self. Are you breathing alone or do you sense your breathing joins you to other living things, other realities? Ask yourself: Who or what is breathing?

This practice is not like the complex breathing practices of yoga or esoteric spiritual traditions. Just as life is simple, this is a simple shift of attention to what already is. The practice is natural, just as we are part of nature. It helps us sense and trust that other forces are moving through us, that we are part of something beyond ourselves, that we are connected. Perhaps most radically, it helps us understand that in our world of effort and willpower, what is most essential is taking place beyond our control. We are not breathing really; rather, something is breathing through us. As we become more aware of this truth, we release our grip on life and give ourselves to the mystery of how life sustains and heals itself.

*And the world cannot be discovered by a journey of miles,
no matter how long, but only by a spiritual journey, a journey
of one inch, very arduous and humbling and joyful, by which we
arrive at the ground at our own feet, and learn to be at home.*

*I can think of no better form of personal involvement
in the cure of the environment than that of gardening. A person
who is growing a garden, if he is growing it organically, is
improving a piece of the world. He is producing something
to eat, which makes him somewhat independent of the
grocery business, but he is also enlarging, for himself,
the meaning of food and the pleasure of eating.*

Wendell Berry

3. GARDENING

It is only late in my life that I have learned to appreciate the rich texture of the soil, how it speaks through the fingers to the soul. I am not by nature a gardener. I do not have "green fingers." The first garden I attempted was a disaster! I was in my early twenties and wanted to be part of the back-to-the-earth/sustainability movement. A friend in South London had a derelict, bramble- and weed-infested backyard, which she offered to me. And so for a few weeks I worked hard, clearing and digging and planting vegetables. I enjoyed the clearing and digging, but the plight of my vegetables was sad. The carrots were tiny, the zucchinis blighted, and the tomatoes I had placed in a row so wrongly-oriented that each plant ended up shading the one behind it. I cannot remember any experience of cooking or tasting the produce from my garden, only the realization that being self-sustaining was not going to be part of my lifestyle or spiritual practice!

But now, almost half a century later, I have found my way back to growing things and have rediscovered the simple mystery of reconnecting with the earth through nurturing plants with my own hands. Now I have a small vegetable garden that I cherish. It is quite recent. Our previous house in the woods beside the ocean did not have a fence, and the deer would come right up to the house, eating everything they could. But recently we moved from amongst the trees and have a fence. Outside the fence we can watch the deer and her young eating the grass and the weeds. Inside the fence we can have flowers and vegetables. It is one of the great pleasures of my old age.

My wife does most of the work in the garden. She understands the magic of the earth and its plants much more than I do. She grows the flowers whose colors take us from winter into spring and are a constant celebration. I love to sit and watch the bees in the lavender and the brilliant green hummingbirds drinking nectar from the flowers.

But now I have also learned to put my fingers into the earth, to plant with attention and care, compost and water, and to watch the vegetables grow. I can sense the sacred alive in the soil and in the simple wonder of what grows, and even in the banana slugs I have to take off the lettuces. I have discovered the simple pleasure of picking vegetables from the garden and bringing them to the kitchen to cook. This act is a return to the great cycles of life from which we are so easily divorced. To go into the garden and pick a cabbage and bring it back to the kitchen, to chop and steam it and eat with butter and salt and pepper is nourishing on so many levels. In that cabbage we have grown and harvested, cooked, and now eaten, I can feel the energy from the earth, the soil, and the sun, and I feel myself as a part of it all— not as an idea, not even as a spiritual practice, but as something even more immediate, as a matter of taste and touch, of my body reconnected to the Earth's body.

Recently I have loved to grow potatoes. I made two new beds for my potatoes, dug and composted, and planted my seed potatoes, and then waited. As I said, I am not a natural gardener, not naturally in tune with the rhythms of the Earth. This has been a gift that life has unexpectedly offered to me—this simple joy in waiting, watching the shoots begin to come from the soil, and then finally putting my fingers in the soil to dig up my potatoes, feeling the wonder of so many potatoes from a single seed. Of course these are not the perfect potatoes bought from the store. These are my own potatoes, cherished because I planted them, and their imperfections do not bother me. I love their taste, sweet and buttery. In my potatoes the Earth has given me more than abundance and nourishment; it has also brought this joy I had never expected—a simple primal joy that is a remembrance of life.

In the fall it is time for tomatoes and zucchini or squash. So much, so many! The blighted garden of my twenties is long forgotten. Maybe it is just that the soil is better, or that I have learned to compost—and of course there is the sunshine here in California rather than the cloudy wet summers of London. But for me it is like a childhood I never had, finding the squash hidden amongst the leaves, growing so quickly. And so many tomatoes! We pick them by the bucketful. Cooking squash and tomatoes together with a few herbs—what more can one want?

This is of course nothing new to any gardener, but for me it has been such an unexpected gift, this sense of natural abundance, this giving and giving of the Earth, this endless generosity. It has made me aware again and again of how much we are given. As much as putting my fingers in the soil or eating my potatoes for supper, this simple awareness of abundance has proved an important reconnection to life. Just to feel and to taste how much we are given is a return to something essential, to a deep knowing how we belong to the Earth.

Of course our small vegetable garden does not fully support us—we also go to the store, especially in the winter months. But to eat what you grow, to taste the soil, to feel the energy that has come from the earth where you live is for me an unexpected blessing. I love to watch a cauliflower slowly developing on the plant—and then it happens so quickly, those white spirals forming in just a few days. It is like being part of a prayer—and of a deep remembering, that this is how it always was, for thousands of years. We are, we have always been, a part of the Earth, fed by the Earth, nourished by Her endless generosity.

GARDENING PRACTICE

Growing plants for food and pleasure has been a sustaining practice for humanity for many thousands of years. Today, with our modern food-production systems and our crowded cities, many of us have lost the intimacy and nourishment that come from working directly with the Earth. But this connection is dormant, like a seed, in all of us, and can easily be awakened by a conscious practice of growing and tending plants. Caring for growing things, even a single houseplant or a pot of herbs on a windowsill, can restore us to our fundamental connection to the Earth and remind us of our place in the intricate interconnectedness of all creation.

A gardening practice grounded in the principles of spiritual ecology rests on the recognition of our participation within the great web of life, in which everything is connected and works in concert with everything else. Gardening enters us into a co-creative relationship with all the elements at play: the plants we grow, the soil, the sun, the water, the temperature and quality of the air, the wind, the rain, the turning of the seasons, the microbes and minerals inhabiting the soil, other plants and insects and animals. Let an understanding of the natural world as a great collaboration in which we participate form the foundation of your gardening practice.

🐚 *In this intricate web* in which everything responds to everything else, it matters what we bring of ourselves to the garden—our touching of the soil, our fingers in the earth, our reaching down into the ground. Be aware of your attitude as you work in the garden. Do you rush through planting, or do you give time to recognize the potential of each seed as you place it into the soil? Do you water and weed out of a sense of obligation, or do you allow the elements to draw you into relationship—the sun to warm you, the rain to soothe you, the earwigs to call you to action? The Earth desperately needs our loving care and attention, our respect, our willingness to listen and engage now, and we can offer these qualities to Her in the attitudes we bring to our gardening.

🐚 *Let your gardening be a conversation*: listen and observe, respond. Allow your garden to tell you what is needed. Put your hand in the steaming compost—is it ready to be mixed with the soil? Watch as the tassels on the corn stalks move with the wind—is it enough to pollinate the kernels? Finger the browning needles on the small fir tree—does it need more shade, or less? Does it need more water? Move through all the stages of the life in your garden with this openness to what is taking place, what is needed from you and what is being given, what in deeper ways may be on offer.

🌿 *Celebrate the harvest*—both the literal harvest and the pleasures that gardening yields along the way. Mimic and amplify the Earth's receptivity in accepting and enjoying what She gives, and Her generosity by sharing Her bounty with others.

Whether we are planting a single rose bush or five acres of wheat, gardening invites us to infuse our deepest qualities into our relationship with the Earth. Respect, awe, admiration, and love nourish us like the food we grow. They also nourish the Earth. The incomparable smell of lavender, the sweetness of an ear of corn, the ragged beauty of a mossy oak, break us out of our shell of isolation if we allow them to. Participating in their care reinforces the innate reciprocity of the Earth—as we nourish Her, She nourishes us.

Everything of the Earth speaks to us. Working in the soil and caring for what grows attunes us to Her language of wholeness.

*And in His hand He showed me a little thing, the quantity of a
hazelnut, in the palm of my hand; and it was as round as a ball.
I looked thereupon and thought; "What may this be?"
And I was answered thus: "It is all that is made."
And I marvelled how it might last, because it was so small.
And I was answered: "It lasteth and shall ever last for that God
loveth it. And everything hath being by the love of God."*

Julian of Norwich

4. SEEDS *and* THEIR STORIES

Working in the garden, planting seeds in the soil, returns me not only to the earth, but also to one of humanity's oldest and most profound stories. The story of the seed planted in the earth—germinating, growing in the darkness, breaking through the surface towards the sunlight—is one of our most ancient stories of fertility. It tells of the mystery of death and rebirth—of the outer, physical rebirth of nature as winter turns to spring, but also of an inner transformation, reminding us that we too can descend into the inner world, the darkness within us, where we can experience the secrets of the soul, a spiritual rebirth.

What I experience in my small garden is part of a story that has held us for millennia. It has given life meaning and sustenance. But today we are losing both our seeds and their stories. The biodiversity that was central to life for thousands of years is being lost. We are becoming a monoculture with a scarcity of seeds, a scarcity so severe that people have even created seed banks in the frozen North to protect our heritage of seed diversity.

When I take my morning walk in later summer I often marvel at an old apple tree whose branches push over the hedge, laden with red and golden fruit. Nature's generosity is one of life's wonders, and yet even this apple tree holds the hidden sadness of loss, reminding me how little remains of what was once a rich diversity. At one time in this country we had around 5,000 apple varieties. Now only 15 varieties account for 90% of apples grown. Accordian, Camack Sweet, Haywood June, and Sally Crocket are just a few of the varieties which have been lost. Like apples, all seeds—our most essential source of sustenance—are losing their biodiversity. They are suffering the same fate as much of the natural world, with many varieties being made extinct: 75% of crop biodiversity lost from the world's fields.[8] The failing of crop diversity is just another example of what our mechanized world is destroying, of the ecocide we are witnessing.

But just as we need to treasure the physical seeds that remain, valuing life's diversity, so do we need to remember the stories that seeds contain. Without these stories of the inner mystery of life and rebirth, of transformation in the darkness, our souls are not nourished and we forget their connection to the Earth and Her rhythms—the seasons of the sacred. We need to keep these stories alive as well; without them we remain stranded in the surface masculine world of science and technology, starved of an inner nourishment essential to our well-being and wholeness.

How can we reclaim these stories, honor their symbols that are as vital to us as the rituals of planting and harvesting? First we need to recognize the value of the symbolic. These stories speak to our soul in the fluid ancient language of images and symbols, a language that points us to the mystery beyond what we think we know and that does not work according to the linear rational logic that dominates our present education and discourse, which captures only one dimension of our lives.

Then we need to remember how to listen, how to be inwardly receptive and attentive. Only from a place of receptivity, the wisdom of the feminine, can we hear the mystery behind the words and images, can we hold their numinous meaning.

When I hold a seed in my hand I am touched by the wonder of it, that something so small tells the story of the soil and the spring, contains the flower, the fruit. All of life seems present, and we know how the story of our own life began with something even smaller, a single cell in the womb. Holding a seed, putting it into the earth, we are back at the beginning, that moment of our own conception, the spark that contains a whole life waiting to be lived. There is a mystical moment in which you experience the seed that contains *all that is*.[9] One night I saw the whole of creation like a seed, like a small round object. Everything, all the oceans and stars, all the trees and people and promises and dreams, were in this small round object. Everything that existed was there. And every small seed, of a flower or vegetable, the pip in the apple that can become a whole tree, is the same, contains the cycle of creation, the stories of humanity and the whole world.

The seed that contains "all that is made" is my own seed story, stamped deep into my soul, binding me to this world through the mystery of love. But from a place of listening, attuned to the deeper mystery of what is sacred, we can each find our own seed story. We each need to find a story that speaks to us, that resonates with our own soul. It might be the simple image of a seed that we plant in the earth, whose shoots then appear in the springtime—the eternal return and promise of new life. Or it could be drawn from the treasure trove of ancient myth, like the richly textured Greek myth of Demeter and Persephone, which tells of the mysteries that belong to the sacred feminine, mysteries that were practiced at Eleusis in Greece for over a thousand years.

It is for each of us to hear and treasure the story that speaks to us,[10] the way the symbol of the seed speaks to us, and to learn to listen to it with an inner ear attuned to symbolic meaning. This is how these stories come alive, and it is one of the reasons that telling and listening to stories is so important. These ancient stories can communicate directly to our inner self in ways our present culture hardly understands.

The images of these stories belong to our heritage, often, as with Persephone, a mystery passed from mother to daughter. Part of the tragedy of our present culture is that all our attention is on the outer, the physical world. And yes, outer nature needs our attention; we need to act before it is too late, before we ravage and pollute the whole ecosystem. We need to save the seeds of life's diversity. But there is an inner mystery to a human being, and this too needs to be rescued from our present wasteland—we need to keep alive the stories that nourish our souls. If we lose these seeds we will have lost a connection to life's deeper meaning. And then we will be left with an inner desolation as real as the outer.

SEED PRACTICE

Every seed is unique. Every plant, every fruit, every flower, is an individual expression of creation. At the same time, the essence of a seed is universal. It is the beginning, the spark, the creative power that enlivens all that is. All of life comes from a seed, from the spiraling galaxies of the Big Bang to the sunflower growing from a seed in a garden pot.

Our own seed stories reflect this truth of microcosm and macrocosm. Every human being contains the essence of what is eternal and sacred. But just as seeds grow to become individual flowers, apples, pears, or oaks, every individual is uniquely herself. To know our own seed story is to live this paradox, that we are both unique and one with the entire universe, we are ourselves as well as an expression of the power within all life. Our lives—our stories—are our own, and yet they are inextricably linked to the stories of others, to the stories of the whales, wolves, pine trees, and snakes, and to the stories of our time.

&~ You can ground this understanding in a concrete way by making a practice of growing plants from seed. How many of us as children grew a sunflower from seed in our primary school classroom, and so experienced this miracle firsthand? First, hold a seed in your hands, and then as you tend to it through all the stages of its evolution—germinating, sprouting, growing, flowering, fruiting, seeding, dying—you can witness this simple wonder: the promise hidden in a seed, and how your caring is a part of it. And so this awareness of the seeds we grow can help move us out of the fragmentation of our times into an experience of life's wholeness.

If you have a garden, try setting aside a few of your plants for the sake of preserving their seeds. Learn the best practices for seed saving and become a steward of seeds. Exchange seeds with fellow gardeners. An awareness of the power and beauty of seeds and their fundamental importance to life, both literal and symbolic, can be a cornerstone for a practice of spiritual ecology. Growing plants for the sake of their seeds can serve as an outward anchor for that understanding and practice—besides contributing to the critical worldwide effort to preserve the diversity of seeds, helping in a small way to take the future of seeds out of the sole hands of commercial interests.

The unfolding life of a seed can also be seen as a metaphor for one's own unfolding story. Our "seed stories" reflect the inner mysteries of life and death as they play out in our lives: our origins and our destinies; our unfolding into what we really are; the universal drama of descent into darkness, transformation, re-emergence and rebirth. What are your seed stories? The seed stories of your community? Of our shared planet? You might find a seed story in the events of your own life or the life around you, in myths, in dreams—the images and symbols that resonate with life's deeper meaning are all around us. Find the stories that speak to you, that allow you to put your own life into a dimension of larger meaning, that nourish your soul. A first step is to find the humility, the ground, the place of vulnerability from which you can truly listen. The word humility comes from the Latin *humus,* which is earth, ground. Just as the seed needs earth to grow, humility is the soil for our own seed stories and the stories of all creation.

Be aware of how you yourself might be a seed—how you might be a part of the unfolding stories of our times, especially the much-needed narrative of humanity coming back to a sacred relationship to the Earth. We are all part of this greater story, and if we pay attention we can find echoes of it in our own lives, sense how this unfolding is living through us, and, with awareness and intention, contribute to its realization in the life around us. Often in spiritual life, it's important to recognize the connection between the inner and the outer, and ask ourselves: Can we find in ourselves the willingness, the capacity, to recognize the signs? To respond from a place of inner truth, of true connection? To honor what is taking place within and around us? Can we see the seeds of this new beginning, of life re-creating itself? How can we nurture this new growth? Life is urgently calling for our awareness and love and humility, to remember that we belong to the Earth, that we are a part of life's sacred wholeness.

An awareness of seeds can take us into the heart of life and into our own hearts. Life will give us opportunity after opportunity to live from our hearts instead of our fears or desires, and over time we can recognize these patterns and work up the courage—the power of the heart, cor—*to respond from a place that is real within us, the place where life has dropped a seed of longing, a seed of truth, a seed of itself. When we live from this inner truth, our lives start to bloom. From here, we recognize the story of the wolf, tell the story of the rain, sing the song of the moon.*

Let dharma be the same as food,
and let food be the same as dharma ...

This food is the fulfillment that is the joy of dharma
and the delight of meditation.

Dogen[11]

5. COOKING *with* LOVE

When I was in my teens and began to practice meditation, I also learned to cook. I have an instinctual belief that to prepare and cook one's food with attention is an essential part of spiritual life that provides a necessary ingredient for the journey. When Dogen, the founder of the Soto Zen school, went to China to rediscover the roots of Zen, his most instructive meeting was with an old monk who was chief cook of the monastery, who rebuked him for not understanding that cooking was a spiritual practice.[12]

Maybe it was this ancient tradition that returned when, along with meditation, I learned to chop vegetables and bake stone-ground bread. I had been brought up without any consciousness of food, in the English style of cooking, in which cabbage is boiled for twenty minutes until all the goodness has long gone. With my chopping board, knives and wok, I learned to bring attention to cooking and eating. It was also an excellent silent rebellion against my middle class family background—while everyone was eating their Sunday lunch of roast beef and roast potatoes, I was sitting at the same table eating a bowl of rice and vegetables with chopsticks!

I learned to cook with awareness, with a sense that food is not just something we eat but also part of a spiritual practice, a sense that cooking and meditation go together, bringing outer and inner purity. Through being attentive to the preparation of our food we bring an awareness into a basic substance and sustenance of life. Just as being aware of the breath is central to spiritual life, reconnecting us with life's essence, so is the simple art of cooking. What is more satisfying than a bowl of rice and vegetables that you have prepared and cooked with attention—what is a greater gift to a visitor and friend?

Then one day in my late twenties, I discovered something very different about cooking. My teacher invited me to a meal she had cooked, simple Indian fritters with rice and chutney. And I tasted love. I had never known that one can taste love, but after that meal my understanding of cooking changed completely. Yes, attention as one chops the vegetables, as one stirs the pot, is vital, but there is another ingredient that adds a totally different dimension to a meal—love.

If in my childhood there was little consciousness about food, there was no awareness of love. And to be given a plate of fritters and rice in which love was the central ingredient and the main taste was revolutionary. Even the idea that one can taste love was something altogether new. Other people may have known this all their lives, known the sweetness of a cake that comes not just from the sugar—but it opened worlds to me.

Is there a technique for cooking with love? I do not know, except that it happens. Maybe it happens when, as with the old cook who taught Dogen, cooking becomes one's "practice of the Way." My teacher had studied with a Sufi master in India and learned the secrets of love, how to work with love. Her cooking was an expression of her training and practice. But from this one meal I learned something so simple and wonderful—that one can put love into food that then nourishes both the body and the soul. This new ingredient now became central to my cooking.

There are wonderful spiritual practices for cooking. One can cook with mindfulness and attention, as in the Zen tradition. One can say a *mantra* or *dhikr* when one prepares a meal, so that the food is infused with remembrance of God.[13] But love is a simple expression of the heart. It does not require special training, only an awareness and offering of the love in one's heart. And the food responds. The food knows that it is loved and it passes on this gift to the one who enjoys the food. A deep sharing then takes place, as if an ancient magic is part of the meal.[14]

So now, when I cook, I remember that meal of rice and fritters, I remember love. Of course sometimes I just make and eat an omelet, grill a piece of fish, and maybe I am not even consciously attentive. But if I am present in my heart as well as my fingers, then love can be present, love can be the secret ingredient of a meal. This is one of the reasons I rarely eat at restaurants. The food may taste good, but this central ingredient is hardly ever present; something essential is missing. And love is what speaks to us, both on a cellular level and in the soul. It nourishes our body on all levels.

How to cook with love is for each of us to discover, because our heart is unique to each of us, just as the song of our soul is unique to each of us. And yet love is also the primary substance of life; it connects us with the divine Source of all that exists. And for me, one meal cooked with love was an experience of a lifetime. Forty years later I can still taste it.

THE PRACTICE *of* COOKING *with* LOVE

Food and love are two of the most vital forms of human nourishment. Combining them is a simple but essential practice.

Love is alive. It is so much more than just the feeling we call love; it is the animating force of life, working according to principles far vaster than our own lives. When we feel it moving, most of us try to grab on to it or chase after it, make it our own. But it is the very nature of love to move and flow. The more it flows, the more it serves. It grows as it is given.

Cooking with love is natural, because through cooking we give. Cooking and serving food is one of the most ancient and basic human gifts. We serve those who eat the food with the Earth's sustenance—Its gift—as well as with our time, effort, care, and attention. Through this gift we are in turn given the opportunity to consciously reconnect with the foundation of life.

🖎 *To practice cooking with love,* begin with the trust and confidence that love is accessible and can be worked with. Without this fundamental understanding, love will not be drawn in, cannot season, or nourish. Cultivate the trust that love is always available to an open heart, and that through our loving attention we can create ways for love to flow.

🖎 *As you prepare to cook,* let your heart open to love. Let yourself feel—love comes in on feeling. A simple

41

way to begin to access love in the kitchen is to cook for people you love—your friends, your family, your partner, the person you're in love with—allowing your feeling for them to infuse the process. We experience love most familiarly in the love we feel for others and from others, the feelings of affinity and affection or passion that bind human beings together. Even if you are cooking just for yourself, you can bring love in, drawing on the same kindness and compassion of love that you would bring to others. This love is not self-regard, but a real, needed nourishment for the body and soul.

But as love animates all of life, it is not limited to our love for one another and ourselves. It can be found everywhere, in everything. It is abundantly present in the ingredients we use in our cooking, and we can access it simply through bringing our open attention to them as we work. Begin by slowing down—don't rush; give yourself time and space to cook. Look closely at the ingredients you are using. Consciously touch and smell them. Recognize the bright beauty of the carrot; the symmetry of a cauliflower; the mysterious, universal swirl of a fiddlehead; the simple wonder of an egg. Breathe in the scent of the herbs and be conscious of their unique properties—how one can revive your liver and another soothe your stomach. Imagine the cow, buffalo, or chicken in the meat, milk, cheese, or eggs you are cooking, acknowledging the living animal whose life has become part of your food. Feel the love from the Earth that has made all this bounty available to you.

🐄 *The love that gives life* to all things also comes alive through your hands. It is accessible through the simple awareness and care you bring to chopping the vegetables, stirring the pot. As you work, bring the feeling from your heart into your hands, from your hands into the food. Love is alive; it wants to flow, and through your attention you can participate in directing its flow.

🐄 *Be attentive to the offering* that this act of cooking is. As you pepper the stew to refine the taste, be aware that you are creating something to give, to feed, and share. Reaffirm the fundamental generosity of the Earth—how It not only keeps us alive but gives us pleasure and enjoyment through our senses of smell and taste, and how through cooking you are participating in that generosity.

In our modern world we have almost entirely lost this direct relationship with food. But food links us together and to the

Earth, and cooking can help us become more conscious of this essential gift of love. Everything that is part of cooking—from the fire of the stove and the herbs we season with, to the water or wine we pour—invites us to consciously participate in this circle of life that both gives and receives. The more we recognize that we are part of this wholeness, not separate from it, the more love can flow with and through us.

The world needs love. It needs love to flow like water, to be breathed like oxygen. Love should be savored, as it nourishes us in hidden ways. Love is like a key ingredient in a recipe that only the grandmothers remember. And yet it is here with us, waiting to be used, simple—like salt on the shelf. It is the most fundamental ingredient of all of life.

Bamboo shadows sweep the stairs,
But no dust is stirred.
Moonlight penetrates the depths of the pool,
But no trace is left in the water.

Nyogen Senzaki

6. CLEANING

There is a simple spiritual practice that is often overlooked —the art of cleaning. The image of the monk sweeping the courtyard has a deep significance, because without the practice of cleaning there can be no empty space, no space for a deep communion with the sacred. Outer and inner cleaning belong to the foundation of spiritual practice, and as the monk's broom touches the ground, it has a particular relationship to the Earth. We need to create a sacred space in order to live in relationship to the sacred within ourselves and within creation.

In today's busy life cleaning one's home is often considered a chore. We may give time and energy (and expensive products) to our daily ritual bathing, but the simple art of cleaning our living space is rarely given precedence. Our culture calls to us to use products that will kill all of the "germs" that surround us, products that are often more toxic than the germs themselves, but do we give attention, mindfulness, to caring for the space in which we live? Are we fully present with our brush or vacuum cleaner?

Once I realized that everything is part of one living whole, that nothing is separate, I understood how everything needs care and attention. I bring this feeling and awareness into my cleaning. Cleaning a table, dusting a shelf, I give attention and love, because everything responds to love and care—not just people, or animals, or plants, but everything. I feel strongly that just as I should only have what I need, I should only have what I can look after, love, and care for. It is a simple recognition of the sacred that is present within everything, and a way to live from the heart in everyday life. Maybe, having been brought up in a family without love or care, I feel this need especially strongly, but I sense that it comes from a deeper knowing of how everything is part of the fabric of love—that creation is woven out of love. And so when I clean I am also looking after, caring for, what is around me, knowing that it too needs to be loved.

I must admit that I love to clean. I find cleaning deeply reassuring. Personally I love emptiness, inner and outer space. In cleaning my living space I am creating emptiness, clearing up the debris that so easily accumulates. And when one cleans with love and attention, one is not vacuuming just the dust, but also the psychic debris, even the worthless thought-forms that stay in the air. Because our culture only values what it can see and touch, we do not understand this invisible accumulation. But it is real, and without conscious attention it clutters our life more than we realize. Just as ritual bathing prepares the worshipper, or just as we may take off our shoes at the entrance to a temple or mosque (or even a friend's home), cleaning is an important preparation for living with the sacred in our daily life.

When I first started lecturing, traveling over America, I would stay in people's houses. At the time I was lecturing mainly to Jungian psychology groups, and so would sometimes stay in the house of a therapist. I remember one night being given a bed in the "spare room," which was also my host's therapy room. After a few restless hours I gave up trying to sleep and realized that I was lying in the psychic soup of all of his patients. Through his therapy work he brought unconscious feelings to the surface, brought shadow-dynamics, anger, and depression into consciousness. And so they were floating around the room, waiting to attach themselves to the next person who entered. The therapist had no understanding of psychic cleaning. Sadly it had not been part of his training or practice. The air was dense with discarded psychic contents.

This is not uncommon. Often people who do healing wash or shake their hands afterward, but then the illness just goes into the water or into the air, to be drunk or breathed by another. When my teacher was in India with her Sufi sheikh, she would sometimes witness him performing a healing. She noticed that after each healing he would cup his hands and bring something to his mouth. She realized that he was inwardly digesting the sickness that he had cleansed, so that it would not just stay in the air and attach itself to another person.

Ecological awareness teaches us the importance of recycling and composting. The waste from our daily lives should not be allowed just to accumulate in a landfill. Nor should it be allowed to get into our water, which in a less visible way is becoming toxic with all the tranquilizers and other drugs that go through our system into the water, affecting and mutating the fish. There are many ecologically aware people who make it a practice to leave as little as possible in their garbage bins for the landfills and work to safeguard the food and water supply, and this is very commendable. But if we are to practice spiritual ecology, if we are to include the spiritual in our ecological awareness, we need to bring a greater awareness to *all* the debris we leave behind. We need to learn how to clear up after ourselves, how to keep an empty space—how to be attentive in our cleaning.

When we bring a quality of attention to our cleaning, the psychic debris can be absorbed along with the dust. Often the attention is linked to the breath, so the two work together.[15] When we work this way the debris does not harm us, and I have found a deep satisfaction in this practice.

Our present culture teaches us to accumulate, but not how to make empty. But for real spiritual work in the inner and outer worlds, in order to give space to the Divine, in order to return to the sacred, we need to practice a certain purification in our daily lives. We learn to eat consciously, to be attentive to our outer environment, to sweep our courtyard. We also need to learn how to clean our house, both physically and inwardly. Just as we need to learn to empty our mind in meditation, to clear away the clutter of unnecessary thoughts, so do we need to consciously clean our living space. Dusting, sweeping, vacuuming with attention, we bring a certain awareness to the ground of our being. This has to do with respect for our environment.

In some old Celtic rituals, after a wedding the couple walk to the celebration preceded by a young boy and girl with brooms, who sweep away the evil spirits so that the couple have a happy marriage. These ancient rituals carry an understanding of the inner worlds and how they can affect our daily life. In the practice of spiritual ecology we are working not just with the outer physical world, but also with the inner worlds, and we need to respect this.[16] We need to relearn how to live lightly, to leave as little debris behind us as we can. We need to relearn how to sweep with our broom. It is simple good housekeeping, more important than we realize.

CLEANING PRACTICE

While many spiritual traditions include the physical purification of diet and fasting, or the inner purification of psychological work, the simple act of cleaning our outer environment is often overlooked. But if we are to bring real presence into our daily life, we need to live in a space we have consciously cleared and emptied. And like many practices, cleaning starts with attention, benefits from discipline, and generates joy.

In our polluted culture, dust and dirt accumulate more quickly than we realize, particularly if we live in a city or beside a road. Without our noticing, the windows become stained, the light no longer shines so brightly into our living space, and a layer of dust creeps into our rooms. Often we no longer notice what we have lost. But through regular attention, we look after where we live, and allow more clarity and light.

&~ *Start by looking* around your house or apartment with an honest, receptive awareness. Are there corners filled with dust or spider webs or areas that simply don't feel good? Go there—clear out the dust and the webs, sweep up the dirt, wash the floor and the items that are there. Make a conscious connection to the spaces and the objects you're cleaning, with the awareness that the sacred is present in everything, that everything, whether animate or inanimate, responds to care and love. Be aware of how the space feels before and after you clean.

🍃 *Be aware of your breath* as you clean, feeling the love that can flow on the breath into your environment, and the living connection the breath makes between inner and outer.

🍃 *Look closely* at the things you have collected over the years. Look in your garage, your closets and cupboards—into the corners you rarely access. Do you own household items that you have not used or appreciated in recent months and years? Have these items and the space around them also accumulated dust and dirt? If so, clean them with caring attention, and then give the neglected objects away to someone who needs them or will truly enjoy and care for them. Do you own clothes or shoes that you have not worn for over a year? Ask yourself why you hang on to them. If there is not a good reason, then give them away. If there is a good reason, keep them and wear them with a new appreciation. Perhaps you can commit to giving away something old every time you bring something new into the house.

🍃 *Try to make it a regular practice* to clear out what you are not using, enjoying, or respecting, and to clean what remains. Set aside a time every week to attend to at least one area of your house or your outdoor space. Keeping a space empty is easier than struggling to clean out dirt or items that have accumulated over years. Or return to the old practice of a "spring clean," when, in celebration of the season and the sun, all the windows were opened, the cupboards were emptied, and the house was cleaned from top to bottom.

🖐 *When you have finished,* take a minute to appreciate the clean space. Through cleaning, we create a space that allows us to see and honor what is present. Notice how the clean wood floor, for example, reveals the grain and the knots of the wood, which tell the story of the forest from which it came. When we clean, we can see all the things of our life present as they are, beyond just our use for them. When cleaning a tile, we can touch and feel the mortar and sense the strength of the stone. When we dust a book, we have respected its pages, the gift of its words. When we wash a window with water, we honor water as cleanser as well as glass as a transmitter of light. Sitting in a room lit by sun pouring through clean windows can feel like sitting inside a diamond. Let yourself receive the gifts a clean space can give back to you.

In a clean space, the inner and outer worlds come together, and relate to each other more directly. We are free to love and care for our surroundings, which hold that love and reflect it back to us. We more easily step into the living whole that nourishes us in so many ways.

Real cleaning is a ritual as simple and essential as paying attention to what we eat, or walking in a sacred manner. It reminds us of where we are, and the importance of looking after the sacred space where we live our everyday life. Cleaning as a practice gives us clarity to see and value ordinary things—that have only too often been stripped of life—as living reflections of the sacred, alive with their own unique qualities and purpose.

Simplicity, patience, compassion.
These three are your greatest treasures.
Simple in actions and in thoughts,
you return to the source of being.
Patient with both friends and enemies,
you accord with the way things are.
Compassionate toward yourself,
you reconcile all beings
in the world.

Lao Tsu

7. SIMPLICITY

The boat people of Southeast Asia, the Moken, have few possessions. They can only carry what they need in their small boats. They also have no word in their language for "worry." But when the tsunami came, they were attentive and watchful of the water; they saw the sea first come high on the beach and then recede far out. They remembered their stories, their myths of what happens to the seas, and so took their boats into deep water and survived the tsunami. The local fishermen did not survive; their boats were destroyed. They did not watch, they were not attentive.[17]

How can we be fully attentive when our lives are cluttered with so many possessions, so many attachments, so many desires? Will we have time to remember the stories, to watch and move our little boat to deeper waters? Or will we be like the local fisherman, inattentive to the need of the moment, sunk by the tsunami of materialism? We live in a culture in which we are constantly bombarded, our attention distracted, no longer just by the "ten thousand things" of the ancient world, but by ten million things. Everything is demanding our attention, wanting us to consume, to buy, to spend our money and our time. And we do not even know the depths and subtleties of this web of consumerism, its powers of deception.

How can we create a space of clarity, of attentiveness? How can we return to what is essential? How can we remember what really matters, what gives meaning and substance to our daily lives? How can we return to a simplicity of life that honors the simplicity of our essential nature, that gives space for the sacred?

First, we have to acknowledge that our whole culture is caught in the grip of unnecessary desires and recognize the poison of accumulation for what it is. We are conditioned and pressured to want more and more—this is the myth of continual economic progress. This myth has become a monster destroying our ecosystem, taking our money and our life energy. It has polluted our consciousness with its slogans and jingles, designed to distort, to manipulate. And we do not even know the power of its dark magic, how much it has us in its grip, feeding us false promises of a better life, assuring us that "things go better" with the purchase of a product. It has saturated every corner of our culture. We are pressured to consume packaged food and even packaged spirituality. We no longer know the ingredients of our lives.

Second, we have to have the strength to say "no." To go against this toxic flow, to resist the power of its empty promises and the corporations behind them, we have to regain an essential simplicity, return to what we need rather than what we think we want. Only then can we begin to hear the music of life, be attentive to the inner and outer need of the Earth. Only then can we become alive with what is sacred and true.

Third, we have to learn to discriminate, to clear our inner and outer clutter. In the classical love story of Eros and Psyche, one of Psyche's almost impossible tasks is to sort a huge pile of seeds. Like Psyche, we have to sort the many things in our life; we have to make conscious what is of value, what we really need.[18] Discrimination is never an easy task. But as Psyche is aided in her task by some willing ants, we too have help, in the form of an instinctual wisdom, a quiet quality, that is present to us if we are paying attention. And it becomes easier after time and practice. As we clear more space in our inner and outer lives, we become more attuned to what is necessary, more aware of the deceptions and false promises of unnecessary "stuff." We see more clearly how our possessions take more than just space, they also take our attention.

Personally I love the old Taoist ways, the ways of the hermits whose spirituality and nature were blended together, their poems a flock of wild geese crossing high in the sky. They lived an essential simplicity that speaks to my soul: their possessions one robe and one bowl, the decoration of their mountain hut "the moon at the window." I have tried to recapture this simplicity in my life, but today we seem to need so many things just to get by. Again and again I have tried to empty my room, especially when I was younger. But family life demanded more and more possessions—many more than needed by a hermit in a hut—though my children would still complain that I threw out too many things.

So over the years I have tried instead to keep an inner simplicity, an empty space in as many moments of the day as is possible. Now I am getting older, once again I feel the tug of this other landscape, a longing for a small cottage and rain-swept hills—maybe the beautiful and bleak Scottish highlands I knew as a child. But my life remains full, though more with people than possessions. So I keep this simplicity as an inner secret, an emptiness that I crave.

Still I have to be careful. I use modern technology: a computer, the Internet, and I love listening to music on an iPod. All around me I feel consumerism and its dark web of desires that so easily entangles us, more than we realize. And often it is not enough to clear out the physical clutter in our homes; we need also to bring a simplicity to how we spend our time, how we use our attention—to be mindful in how we live.

The practice of meditation and mindfulness can clear the clutter of our minds. A few trips to the goodwill or charity store can clear the clutter from our homes. And then continual attention is needed so that the currents of accumulation do not fill the empty space we have created.

And beyond the clutter of thoughts and things, we also have to watch that we are not caught in constant activity, our culture's emphasis on endless "doing" rather than "being." We need space in order to watch, to listen, to walk, to breathe—to be present. The *Tao Te Ching* teaches the value of not doing:

> Less and less is done until nothing is done,
> When nothing is done, nothing is left undone.

Through a quality of emptiness we can access a deeper rhythm than the surface jangle of constant activity. We used to be held by the rhythms of the seasons and the soil. Now we have to struggle to return to a rhythm and a space that are not toxic with consumption, that belong to the seasons of the sacred, where life still flows true to its essential nature. Simplicity, patience, and compassion can guide and keep us inwardly aligned. Gradually we can once again listen to the Earth, to Her wisdom and beauty; we can feel the beating of both Her heart and ours. We can feel again the deep belonging that allows us to be present in every moment, not as a practice but a simple state of being. We can remember why we are here.

SIMPLICITY PRACTICE

Simplicity is the essence of life. The word itself comes from the Latin simplex, *meaning uncompounded or composed of a single part. Simple things reflect this essential nature, which belongs to everything in creation. When we honor the simple things of life, we bring ourselves back to this oneness, our true Home.*

All the practices in this book are a return to simplicity. Breathing, walking, growing food, cooking … these are the "chop wood, carry water" of our day. If we honor what is essential in our lives, we connect with the life force that runs free of the dramas of our individual and collective psyche. Here we are connected and responsive.

&~ *Begin by giving* extra attention to your simple daily activities, like rising from bed and putting two feet on the floor. Pause there. You are awake; you are alive. Take note of how you feel in your body, and how your feet touch the floor. Be aware as you move towards the bathroom, towards the kitchen and the coffee or tea. Be grateful for water in the sink, for oranges that made your juice, for milk in your tea. Drink slowly. Appreciate your food. Appreciate your family, the sun coming in the window, the beauty you see in your partner or children. Simplicity reveals itself through slowness, in quiet moments when you can see, feel, taste, touch. Take time during the day to stop rushing. Move through the day with respect and openness.

🌿 *Take an honest inventory* of your life. Look at the things you have that take up time and psychic space. Look at your activities and commitments. What of these things do you actually need? Which are habits and entanglements that take up space and weigh you down? Which reflect your real values, feed your soul, touch you with love? Do you need or just want that new thing, that new activity, that has caught your eye? For a short time, try going without some of the things of your life. Maybe you don't need them after all.

🌿 *Let nature teach you.* In nature, we are students of simplicity. The way a tree grows towards the sun, the way a cat stretches beside the fire, the way the seasons come round again and again without fail, can teach the simplicity of what is. The essential nature of our own lives—the cycle of birth, death, suffering and joy, and even liberation—also reflects this simplicity. We might make our lives complicated by how we relate to these—fighting death, avoiding suffering, searching for freedom and happiness—but that is our superimposed experience, not what is. Look for ways to attune to the natural simplicity of life that underlies the complications of our human experience.

🖎 *Bring yourself back* again and again to what is simple, to what does not change over time, to what shines steady through the fog. Ask yourself, do we need more than these things? Do we need more than the beauty of a crab apple tree in spring, a warm house in the winter, the way water sounds flowing through a stream, a cup of tea with friends? Do we need more in our lives than love?

Practicing simplicity doesn't mean giving away all our things, quitting our demanding jobs, and moving to a mountain hut or living off the grid. It simply means being very honest about what we value within our lives, what sustains us, brings us joy and meaning, and devoting ourselves to those activities, people, or things. While we might end up having fewer possessions or changing some of our habits, simplicity compels a return, not a rejection—a seeing through and within, rather than looking somewhere else. When we live from a place of simplicity we naturally find we need less, and instead are more open to life.

Don't be afraid of simplicity. It can feel stark and empty because it is free of psychological complexity and the coverings of accumulated need and desire. But our attention and our genuine response—awe, gratitude, appreciation, and respect—help transform that starkness into the richest of human experiences.

I am bewildered by the magnificence
of your beauty,
and wish to see you
with a hundred eyes....

I am in the house of mercy,
and my heart
is a place of prayer.

Rumi

8. PRAYER

Prayer is our heart crying, our soul invoking. When we kneel on the ground in prayer we touch the invisible world of the spirit, we speak to what we cannot see. Listening in prayer, we open to an intangible presence—our heart, our mind, our soul, and our senses attentive. Prayer is our communion with the Divine that is always all around us and within us.

In our world of action, of relentless doing and fixing, it is easy to underestimate the power of prayer. But since the beginning human beings have prayed, as the simplest and most natural way to communicate with the Divine. Prayer was also fundamental to our connection with and participation in the natural world. In the earliest cave paintings in France, our hunter-gatherer ancestors painted invocations to the spirits of animals, while the first farmers prayed for the rains to come and the crops to grow. There is a legend that when the Hopi people came to America they traveled to the North and South, the East and West, until they settled in the most inhospitable desert, because they knew that they would have to have "a heart full of prayer" for the rains to come and water their corn.[19] Then they could never forget the Divine. Prayer and the natural world have been bonded together since the beginning.

There are many ways to pray, from invoking the spirits of the land, like the protector deities of mountains or the *devas* of plants, to calling to a single transcendent God. In my own experience the Divine is both immanent and transcendent: embodied in everything we can see and touch, closer to us than our breath, than our hands and feet—and also beyond all that exists and does not exist, "beyond even our idea of the beyond." And our prayers can speak to and reach both aspects, the Divine within and the Divine beyond all, through the mystery of the heart.

The heart's witness of the Divine—listening, watching, being fully attentive within the heart, becoming receptive in our whole being—is a profound way of attuning ourself to the sacred. As Rumi writes,

> Make everything in you an ear, each atom of your being, and you will hear at every moment what the Source is whispering to you, just to you and for you, without any need for my words or anyone else's.

You are—we all are—the beloved of the Beloved, and in every moment, in every event of your life, the Beloved is whispering to you exactly what you need to hear and know. Who can ever explain this miracle? It simply is. Listen and you will discover it every passing moment.[20]

Watching, listening, we develop the ear of the heart, the eye of the heart, the inner receptivity of the soul. And if we can listen to the Beloved within creation, to the miracle of the Earth in all Her forms, we will hear the Beloved speak to us as She spoke to our ancestors. We will find ourself in a world as whole as it is holy.

My own morning walk is in many ways a prayer. In prayer there is a meeting: I meet and bow before the One in Its many colors, sounds, and smells. Of course, many mornings I forget and take my own thoughts with me on my walk. But then I am reminded—hearing the waterfowl call across the water, glimpsing the sun through the fog—and I awake from myself and see more clearly—the colors, the sounds, the beauty, the Divine. Once more I am attuned to how "The world is charged with the grandeur of God."

I feel that there is a specially pressing need at this time to bring our heart's witness to this natural world we live in. Our world is starving, dying from a lack of the sacred, and human beings have always been mediators between the worlds, linking matter and spirit, the visible and invisible. Our witness, our prayers, can help awaken the sacred that is within creation.

And there is another form of prayer that touches me deeply at this time of the Earth's distress. With our own heart we can pray for the Earth, just as we pray for another person, for a sick relative or friend. It helps first to acknowledge that She is not "unfeeling matter" but a living being that has given us life, and to open our heart to Her suffering: the physical suffering we see in the dying species and polluted waters, the deeper suffering of our collective disregard for Her soul and sacred nature. And then from this depth of feeling, and a deep love for the Earth, I place the whole Earth in my heart and offer Her to God, to the Creator, to my own Beloved. It is a simple and powerful way of remembering the Earth in my prayers, an offering of love.

We each have our own way to pray, the way we cry out in our need and longing, the way we listen to the quiet voice or to the deepening silence of the Divine, the way we open our hearts to the Earth. There are so many ways to pray for and with creation, to listen within and include the Earth in our spiritual practice. Watching the simple wonder of a dawn can be a prayer in itself. Or when we hear the chorus of birds in the morning we may sense that deeper joy of life and awake to its divine nature, while at night the stars can remind us of what is infinite and eternal within us and within the world. In whatever way we are drawn to wonder or pray, what matters is always the attitude we bring to this intimate exchange: whether our prayers are heartfelt rather than just a mental repetition. It is always through the heart that our prayers are heard. Do we really feel the suffering of the Earth, sense Her need, hear the cry of the Earth? Do we feel this connection with creation, how we are a part of this beautiful and suffering being? Then our prayers are alive, a living stream that flows from our heart. Then every step, every touch, will be a prayer for the Earth, a remembrance of what is sacred. We are a part of the Earth calling to Her Creator, crying in Her time of need.

PRAYER PRACTICE

Prayer is a place of meeting. In the privacy of the heart we can be present with the Divine in our deepest needs and our deepest feelings. In essence it is a communion. In the silence of our being we ask and receive, we witness what is holy.

Prayer is a quality of attention within the heart. It begins with an inner emptiness and listening. Once one establishes this attention, prayer can be anything that speaks to us in the language of the sacred. Prayer can be love or longing, gratitude or praise. It can be an interior response to the beauty of a hummingbird's wings, the taking in of moonlight shining through the window, or the simple placing of a foot on the ground with love or mindfulness. It can be the still small voice of the Divine speaking to us, or something silent and unnameable that arises from a deep place of mystery. Prayer can be a call and it can be an answer, and a dance between the two.

Prayer rests on the capacity to listen, receive, and express from the heart. So while we can pray anywhere and at any time, to start a practice it can be helpful to set a special time early in the morning or in the evening, when the busyness of the day is at bay, and our mind is more naturally calm, when our heart can be open.

🌿 *The practice of prayer* begins with a turning within and an intentional clearing of an inner space. Just as we need to clean and empty the outer spaces we live in in order to keep our attention free, to bring undistracted attention to prayer we need to empty our inner landscape—clear out the thoughts, ideas, emotions, and tensions that carry us on the surface of our lives. This means clearing away even any idea of what "prayer" is or should be. Focusing on the breath can help with this emptying. A simple technique is to imagine any distracting thoughts or feelings flowing out on the out-breath, and on the in-breath to return the attention inward. In the emptiness within we can begin to attune to the depths.

🌿 *Real prayer comes* from the heart—in the words of the orthodox monk Theophan the Recluse: "The concentration of attention in the heart—this is the starting point of prayer." To bring yourself into your heart it can be helpful to consciously bring attention into your chest, where the heart resides, and allow your attention to settle there. Become aware of the heart as a seat of consciousness and intention.

🌿 *In the depths* of the heart we find the holy essence that is the source of all prayer. From here, we can offer the ritual sacred words that we call "prayers."

Or we can allow prayer to be spontaneous: we can honor what emerges, what we hear, feel, sense; we can welcome what comes. Or we might begin with an intention—such as praying for healing for a sick friend or for the Earth, for peace for someone who is suffering, or peace in the strife-ridden world we live in, or for understanding in a difficult situation —and then offer this intention to the heart. Or we can just be present in the inner sanctuary of the soul, in its waiting stillness. Prayer is essentially the heart's conversation with the holiness at the heart of everything. A regular practice of prayer, whatever form it might take, keeps the conversation going, keeps us in the presence of the sacred.

Prayer is a miracle. It opens the doorway of the heart to an infinite universe. Try not to limit prayers with expectations, for prayer is ultimately how we go beyond such limitations. Sometimes a listening silence is the deepest response to our prayers. One Sufi saint was asked, "Why does God not answer my prayers?" He replied, "Because He is listening to you." It is the heart's cry, love's communion, that really matters.

Today, it is especially important to include the Earth in our prayers, to allow our hearts the space to witness the Earth as a living being. Too many of us have forgotten how close we are to Her—that we breathe Her, we eat Her, we share Her body, we dissolve into Her at death. Allow Her to be in your prayers, bring Her into your heart, ask Her heart to welcome you.

In prayer, we live this potential of merging, of dissolving, and reforming. In prayer, is it our self we come to meet? Is it life? Is it the Divine? It is One, in the dynamic flux of the heart that embraces all.

(i who have died am alive again today,
and this is the sun's birthday;this is the birth
day of life and of love and wings:and of the gay
great happening illimitably earth)

E. E. Cummings

9. DEATH

Life and death belong together. One cannot fully say "yes" to life unless one also says "yes" to dying. And yet we live in a culture that tries to insulate us from death. We do not witness the deaths of the animals we eat, and we often isolate our old people during their final months, separating them from the community and their family. Instead of facing the reality of death, we try to perpetuate the myth of eternal youth, in which we have to be youthful and active until our final days, while cosmetic surgeons nip and tuck faces into distorted images that do not naturally wrinkle and grow old. We are always hoping to hold on to something whose very nature is a flow, a movement. Can we not be open to the mystery of death at this time of transition? Many friends have told me how deeply meaningful it has been to be present at the passing of a loved one.

We are surrounded by a natural world that tells us constant stories of death, from a leaf falling in autumn to a hawk plummeting from the sky to kill a small rodent. Just this morning I saw a downy young owl lying dead beside the path. And in my garden flowering and death belong together. The cauliflower that I pick and cook is a flowering that heralds the end of a cycle. Death follows fruition, and as Shakespeare said about death, "Ripeness is all." Isolated from death, we are also isolated from life, from its cycles that give meaning, and from the deeper rhythms of the soul that are echoed in nature.

Nature does not need a facelift. She is eternally young because she is always dying. She is the hundred-year-old tree falling in a thunderstorm as well as the first shoots of spring. The Japanese understood this quality of the sacred, building their temples in wood and not stone so that they would have to be rebuilt again and again.

If we can watch and listen to what life is trying to tell us, what the Earth says in so many ways, then we can bring this mystery of death into our everyday life. On the spiritual path one learns how to let things die, how to let things fall away. One comes to understand the principle of change and impermanence, and how to be present in life in all of its stages. We let our childhood fall away, then our romantic dreams; even our spiritual dreams are allowed to die as we struggle to break free from the cocoon of life's many illusions. The real wisdom is being aware when a cycle is complete, when a stage of life's journey has come to an end, has come to fruition.

Again and again we inwardly die and are reborn. The many coverings of our true self are peeled away, like the skins of an onion. The Sufis say, "Nothing is possible in love without death," because they know that for the heart to break open and embrace the vastness of the Divine, the ego has to "die," to lose its grip. The ego has so many identities, so many false images of itself, all of which have to die if we are going to glimpse and then live what is sacred and true. And this is not a single happening, but a dying that is repeated many times. Winter follows autumn, in the soul as in the natural world. The soul too has its seasons.

In this time when our culture tries to sanitize life and insulate us from death, it is vital that we give death back to life. Only then can we recognize and live the awareness that we are part of this vast pattern of life and death that is also beyond life and death. The eternal is found not just in heaven, but also in the constant change of life. And the Earth is here to teach us this, if we dare to listen, if we dare to be fully present and hear Her stories, watch the constant flow of life and death that is all around us.

My own journey has taken me through many deaths; more has fallen away than I like to remember. Some deaths have been painful, agonizing transitions, some simply a joyous opening of the heart. Again and again I have embraced dying, again and again been born, into a new awareness, a new way of being. Some dying has taken me closer to physical life, to the Earth, to feeling spring under the soil, while some has taken me into the world of spirit—to the other side where I have walked with the angels. I know how close we are to the world of spirit, how it touches us even if we do not notice. Sometimes I long to be fully free of the physical, not just in meditation or prayer, to fully dissolve in the light that is waiting, but then I am drawn back by a glimpse of Earth's beauty, a spider's web in the early morning dew. For me life and death belong together, as friends, as lovers. I cannot image life without the promise of death, of a new beginning, the miracle of being reborn.

In order to return to an inner and outer relationship to the Earth, we need to embrace the mystery of death, told every year in the story of the seed. One cannot have rebirth without death. To return to the sacred is to return to death, and to awaken to the truth that death is a transition, a transformation. In the seed growing in the darkness, in the caterpillar that builds a cocoon to become a butterfly, the Earth tells Her stories of the sacred. And as much as they are the stories of Her journey, so are they our stories, and stories of our journey together.

We live at a time when our culture appears to be dying even as it tries to promise us eternal youth. Cut off from its roots in the Earth, and from any sense of the sacred, it is destroying its own ecosystem with pathologically unsustainable materialism. If we are to be fully present at this time, to help the Earth in this transformation, we need to welcome both death and birth, both winter and spring. Once we understand how interconnected we are, both physically and spiritually—how our body is part of the body of the Earth, our soul part of Her soul—then we can glimpse how our spiritual awareness, a spirituality grounded in the sacred within creation, can help the Earth make this shift. Many species are dying, and this will continue for decades. We cannot escape this sixth mass extinction, the first caused primarily by human beings.[21] But we can participate in a new story being born, a new awareness that once again recognizes our sacred unity. How this story will come into being and evolve we do not yet know—now we see around us many signs of death and only a few shoots of rebirth. But we can say "yes" to this new unfolding. We can be part, even co-creators, of this new story of the Earth.

Just before and at the time of death, a special grace is given to a human being to make the transition beyond life. Many people feel this grace as a certain quality of peace, or even light, in the presence of a dying person. Of course not every death is like this; many people "rage against the dying of the light." But for those who say "yes," the grace is given as a gift. At this time of transition for the Earth, when so many of Her species and so much of Her beauty and wonder are dying, there is also a grace that is present. It is for those who are attuned to the Earth to feel this grace and learn to work with it—be present with the mystery and wonder of the Earth in the inner and outer worlds, and respond with what is needed.

DEATH PRACTICE

Awareness of death is a spiritual practice almost as foundational as awareness of breath. The Sufi dervish meditates throughout the night in a graveyard to conquer his fear of death, Tibetan monks dance the "skeleton dance" in honor of impermanence and transformation, while the Christian monk contemplates a skull as a memento mori, *a remembrance of mortality.*

Death is as sacred as birth. It awakens us. It opens us to the unknown, to one of life's greatest mysteries, and thus it reflects into our lives a reckoning of what truly matters. Today, a death practice that reminds us of impermanence and prepares us for transformation can help us participate at this time in our collective history, as our global civilization commits a mass extermination of species and at the same time gives birth to a new story of life's interdependence.

The key to a death practice is presence. Our culture may turn away from death, but we need to be aware of death and be present with it. We can reflect on the small deaths in our inner and outer life, and on our willingness to let go of attachments, relationships, or patterns of identity. How freely do we go with the changes of life? How much do we cling to what no longer serves?

🍂 *We can also bring* our practice of loving attention to people who are ill or dying. Many of us have friends or family who are facing death either from illness or simply growing old. Be with them. Don't bring an agenda other than to be present and available. Being present with someone who is dying draws us into one of life's greatest transformations, alive with both struggle and grace. Often people suffer as they approach death, either from physical pain or the psychic pain of being out of control and of losing what they thought mattered most. There may be little we can do to help; but with an open heart we can share this existential moment, and feel the potentials of surrender—the peace and grace that help the dying accept the magnitude of what is taking place. Death is always transformation; what is important is whether we welcome and honor this rite of passage.

🍂 *Witnessing the suffering* of the dying is tremendously powerful, for in their suffering we are compelled to come to terms with our own fear of surrender, of trusting something beyond our intellect, of facing how we have spent our lives. Bring death to your own life by asking yourself: If I knew I was dying, how would I spend the time I had left, the days, weeks, or months that remain? What holds the most meaning? What would I regret from the past? Allow your answers to support changes in how you spend your time, what you value, what you invest in. Let go of old habits; create space for what actually supports you and life itself, what really matters.

🐚 *We can also bring our awareness* to the Earth and the myriad animal and plant species that are dying or in danger of dying. Allow yourself to acknowledge and feel the suffering and the death taking place to the Earth, to animals and plants, to the oceans and the air. Feel in your heart the grief and acknowledge the killing—the poisoning, the desecration, the losses—that happens every day. Don't scan quickly through your Facebook feed as you see that yet another pod of whales has washed ashore, dead, from unknown causes. While reading the paper, pay attention to the small stories about another butterfly or frog species dying off, the state of our bee populations, the decimation of another forest for mining. Pay attention, feel what is happening to the Earth in your own neighborhoods and cities. Allow your heart to ache. Only when we fully face and truly feel our loss and our grief can we open the way to the new life that awaits us.

🖎 *Ask yourself:* How can I let death become part of my life? How can the presence of death help me to live more fully, more in touch with the Source? What am I holding on to that contributes to my suffering and the suffering of others? How can I let go and become part of what is being born?

The river is moving fast. Some of us are clinging to the shore or drowning in back-eddies of meaningless and outdated personal and cultural patterns. Others are leaving behind what does not support the continuing journey—relationships, hopes, habits. Don't be afraid of death and the mystery that it echoes into our lives. We need to feel the enormity of what is taking place in the world today—the joy, freedom, and pain—in order to access the power and grace that are guiding this collective death and our birth as well.

You've traveled up ten thousand steps in search of the Dharma.
So many long days in the archives, copying, copying.
The gravity of the Tang and the profundity of the Sung
make heavy baggage.
Here! I've picked you a bunch of wildflowers.
Their meaning is the same
but they're much easier to carry.

Hsu Yun (Empty Cloud)[22]

10. MEANING *and the* SACRED

Waking early, hearing an owl call from the trees, I feel part of something stretching out all around me, a deep vein of life's meaning running through all that exists. How could I live without this heartbeat, this feeling of connection? Life speaks to me in so many ways: from a simple human exchange at the post office counter or at the bakery—a smile, a hello—to the evening clouds forming and reforming, pink against the setting sun. This is real meaning woven into my days—life's story telling itself anew every day. It is the sacred alive in every moment.

We are surrounded by the sacred; it is in the core of our being and in the Earth's. It is the essential nature of everything that is. The "sacred" is not something primarily religious, or even spiritual. It is not a quality we need to learn or to develop. It belongs to the primary nature of all that is.

When our ancestors knew that everything they could see was sacred, this was not something taught but instinctively known. It was as natural as sunlight, as necessary as breathing, a fundamental recognition of the wonder, beauty, and divine nature of the world. From this sense of the sacred real meaning is born, the meaning that makes our hearts sing with the deepest purpose of being alive.

Tragically, our present culture appears to have lost sight of this vital quality. Instead we live on the surface, separated from the real substance that has always given everyday life a depth of meaning. We are told to find meaning in our individual life, but all around us life itself tells us a different story—that we are part of the Earth, that we belong to the community of all of life in its myriad forms. Only through recognizing and living this sacred unity can we find and experience the real meaning that life is offering to us. And so we have to find ways to remember, to reconnect, to feel again what is all around us.

Meaning is what calls from the depths of the soul. It is the song that sings us into life. Whether we have a meaningful life depends upon whether we can hear this song, this primal music of the sacred. Sadly, today so much of life is covered in distractions, in the addictions of consumerism. Just as the infinite majesty of the stars has become hidden by the lights from our cities, the soul's music is being drowned out amidst life's constant clamor. Wonder and mystery have become less and less accessible. As a culture we seem to have lost the thread that connects the inner world, from which meaning is born, to the outer world, where we spend our days. The stories of the soul are no longer told. Instead, our dreams have become the desires of materialism. Even spirituality is often sold in the marketplace, another drug that promises to placate us, to cover the growing anxiety that something essential is missing.

To find meaning we have to reclaim our sense of the sacred, something our culture appears to have overlooked or forgotten. The sacred is an essential quality of life. It connects us to our own soul and the Divine that is the source of all that exists. The sacred can be found in any form: a small stone or a mountain, the first cry of a newborn child and the last gasp of a dying person. It can be present in a loaf of bread, on a table, waiting for a meal, and in the words that bless the meal. The remembrance of the sacred is like a central note within life. Without this remembrance something fundamental to our existence is missing. Our daily life lacks a basic nourishment, a depth of meaning.

When we feel this music, when we sense this song, we are living our natural connection with the Earth and all of life. Meaning is not something that belongs to us. Rather, our life becomes "meaningful" when we live this connection, when we feel it under our feet as we walk down the street, in the scent of a flower, in rain falling. I am very fortunate in that I live in nature. Early each morning as I walk, sensing the day awakening, I feel this simple connection: how the Earth breathes together with me, how It speaks the language of the soul and of life's mystery. Here meaning is as simple as apple blossoms breaking open; as a young hawk, its feathers still downy; as the fog lifting across the water.

The chapters and practices in this small book are simple ways to reconnect so that we can once again feel the music, the song of our living connection with the Earth. They encourage us to slow down, to listen, to sense, to feel, and to be attentive. They draw our awareness from fantasies and desires to what *is*, where meaning waits. There are of course many other ways we can reawaken to the sacred in everyday life, feel the meaning that is present in everything, like blood flowing through us and through the Earth. As Rumi says, "there are a thousand ways to kneel and kiss the ground." It is this sacred ground that is calling to us, that needs our living presence, our attentiveness.

We are all part of one living being we call the Earth, who is magical beyond our understanding. She gives us life and Her wonder nourishes us. In Her being the worlds come together. Her seeds give us both bread and stories. For centuries the stories of seeds were central to humanity, myths told again and again—stories of rebirth, life re-creating itself in the darkness. Now we have almost forgotten these stories. Stranded in our separate, isolated selves, we do not even know how hungry we have become. We have to find a way to reconnect with what is essential—to learn once again how to walk in a sacred manner, how to breathe with awareness, cook with love and prayers, how to give attention to simple things. We need to learn to welcome life in all its colors and fragrances, to say "yes" again and again. Then life will give us back the connection to our own soul, and once more we will hear its song. Then meaning will return as a gift and a promise. And something within our own heart will open and we will know that we have come Home.

NOTES

1. It is very similar to the Sufi practice of "Wheresoever you turn, there is the face of God."

2. The great Sufi Ibn 'Arabi writes about how "... all that exists was born from the hidden depths of the secret meaning of this word *kun*." He describes a vision of the whole universe as a Tree: "... and the life-giving sap running in its veins, the power making it grow and give flowers and fruits is the realm of the uncreated ... where the secret of the word *kun* is hidden." From Ibn 'Arabi, *The Tree of Being*, trans. Shaykh Tosun Bayrak, pp. 90 and 100.

3. "Deep Breathing," Shen Hu Xi and Kenneth Cohen, quoted from *Meditations for InterSpiritual Wisdom*, ed. Netanel Miles-Yepez, 2011, p.148.

4. It is *chi* in Taoism, *prana* in Hinduism, *ruah* and *ruh* to Judaism and Islam, *pneuma* to Christians.

5. Baha ad-Din Naqshband, from the first of the Eleven Naqshbandi Principles.

6. Interestingly some Sufi teachings describe the reverse, that the in-breath brings us into the world of creation and the out-breath returns us to the Source: "The final expiring [i.e., the last out-breath of someone at the point of death] symbolizes the realization of the Immutability which underlies the illusory vicissitudes of creation and dissolution, the realization of the truth that 'God was and there was naught else beside Him. He is now even as He was.'" Quoted by Martin Lings, *A Sufi Saint of the Twentieth Century*, p. 159.

7. This is similar to the Taoist use of breath to increase *chi*, and thus bring healing as well as general well-being.

8. UN Food and Agriculture Organization, quoted in *The Economist*, March 12, 2012.

9. This is echoed in Ibn 'Arabi's vision of the Tree of Being that grew from the seed shed when Allah said *"Kun!"* ["Be!"]. See *The Tree of Being*, p. 91.

10. There are many other seed stories, like the parable of the seeds in Matthew 13, or the Apache legend in which turkey provides people with the first corn and squash seeds.

11. "The Dharma of Taking Meals," quoted by Shohaku Okumura, *Living by Vow: A Practical Introduction to Eight Essential Zen Chants and Texts,* p. 89.

12. Dogen asked the old cook: "Why are you, a person of advanced age, engaged in such a troublesome task as the chief cook rather than in practicing *zazen* or reading the *koans* of old masters? Is there any worthwhile thing in your work?" To this question the old monk laughed loudly and said: "You, a good man from a foreign country, perhaps do not understand what the practice of the Way is ..." From *Eihei Dogen: Mystical Realist,* Hee-Jin Kim, p. 27.

13. The same can be done with sewing or knitting. Then the fabric and thread or the yarn is also infused with divine remembrance —a real gift to the wearer.

14. The story "Babette's Feast," by Isak Dinesen, is a beautiful tale of what can happen to a meal when cooking becomes magical.

15. In the Sufi practice we work with the heart, and so darkness and debris are also absorbed through the heart, with love. Sufis are sometimes known as "sweepers" because they sweep up the debris, the dust of the world, that others leave behind.

16. By "inner worlds" I mean those worlds that are invisible to our physical sight but exist in other dimensions of reality: e.g., the angelic world, the world of the *devas* and nature spirits, the archetypal world of symbols, the inner world of the soul and world soul (the *anima mundi*). Shamans, mystics, and seers, among others, have traditionally had access to different inner worlds.

Sadly, one of the greatest censorships of our Western culture has been to deny the existence of these inner worlds. This has been partly caused by scientific rationalism, but also by the Catholic Church, which persecuted those who had direct access to inner worlds, like the Gnostics.

17. Before the 2005 tsunami that caused so much loss of life, the nomadic Moken sailors who live among the islands in the Andaman Sea, off Myanmar (Burma), recognized the signs of the coming disaster in the dolphins and other fish suddenly swimming to deeper water. So they too took their boats further from the shore and rode out the waves, unlike the Burmese fishermen who were not attentive to the signs of nature but stayed close to shore where they perished as their boats were wrecked by the tsunami. The Moken said of the Burmese fishermen, "They were collecting squid, they were not looking at anything. They saw nothing, they looked at nothing. They don't know how to look."

18. In this love story of classical mythology, Aphrodite gives Psyche a series of seemingly impossible tasks. In *She: Understanding Feminine Psychology*, Robert Johnson gives a simple and profound interpretation of this story in relation to feminine psychology.

19. Hopi farmers traditionally do not use irrigation but "dry farming," which is truly an "act of faith that is dependent on hard work, humility, care, and sincere prayer to provide enough rain to nourish their crops." Rosanda Suetopka Thayer, *The Observer*.

20. *Light upon Light*, trans. Andrew Harvey, p. 99. In his encyclical *On Care for our Common Home*, Pope Francis quotes a Sufi mystic who articulates a similar awareness of listening to the Divine within everything. Ali al-Khawas writes: "There is a subtle mystery in each of the movements and sounds of this world. The initiate will capture what is being said when the wind blows, the trees sway, water flows, flies buzz, doors creak, birds sing, or in the sound of strings or flutes, the sighs of the sick, the groans of the afflicted ..." (p. 168n).

21. In recent years multiple scientific reports have confirmed the Earth has now entered a new extinction phase, its sixth great mass extinction event, with accelerated species depletion due to pollution and destruction of natural habitat. This era, called the Anthropocene, marks a time during which human activity has been the dominant influence on climate and the environment.

22. "Searching for the Dharma," *Six Poems by Hsu Yun*, See: www.hsuyun.org.

ACKNOWLEDGMENTS

For permission to use copyrighted material, the author gratefully wishes to acknowledge: Andrew Harvey, for permission to quote from *Light upon Light*; Counterpoint Press, for permission to quote from *The Unforeseen Wilderness: Kentucky's Red River Gorge*, copyright© 1991 by Wendell Berry, and to quote from *The Art of the Commonplace: The Agrarian Essays of Wendell Berry*, copyright © 2002 by Wendell Berry; and Liveright Publishing Corporation, for permission to quote lines from "i thank You God for most this amazing". Copyright 1950, © 1978, 1991 by the Trustees for the E. E.Cummings Trust. Copyright © 1979 by George James Firmage, from *Complete Poems: 1904-1962 by E. E. Cummings*, edited by George J. Firmage.

ABOUT THE AUTHORS

LLEWELLYN VAUGHAN-LEE, Ph.D., was born in London in 1953 and has followed the Sufi path since he was nineteen. In 1991 he moved with his family to Northern California and founded The Golden Sufi Center (www.goldensufi.org). Author of several books, he has specialized in the area of dreamwork, integrating the ancient Sufi approach to dreams with the insights of modern psychology. Since 2000 the focus of his writing and teaching has been on spiritual responsibility in our present time of transition, and an awakening global consciousness of oneness. More recently he has written about the feminine, the *anima mundi* (world soul), and spiritual ecology (www.workingwithoneness.org). He has been interviewed by Oprah Winfrey on *Super Soul Sunday*, and featured on the *Global Spirit* series shown on PBS.

HILARY HART is the author of three books about mysticism with a focus on women and feminine consciousness. She has been on the Sufi path since 1998. Originally from New England, Hilary currently lives in Taos, New Mexico. Her previous books include *Body of Wisdom: Women's Spiritual Power and How It Serves* and *The Unknown She: Eight Faces of an Emerging Consciousness*.

ABOUT THE PUBLISHER

THE GOLDEN SUFI CENTER publishes books, video, and audio on Sufism and mysticism. A California religious nonprofit 501(c)(3) corporation, it is dedicated to making the teachings of the Naqshbandi Sufi path available to all seekers.

THE GOLDEN SUFI CENTER
P.O. Box 456 · Point Reyes Station · CA · 94956-0456
tel: 415-663-0100 · fax: 415-663-0103
www.goldensufi.org

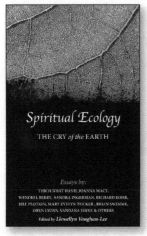

DARKENING *of the* LIGHT
Witnessing the End of an Era

by Llewellyn Vaughan-Lee

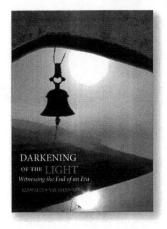

"I BOW TO THE COURAGE IN THIS BOOK. Here Llewellyn Vaughan-Lee has allowed himself to hear the cry of the Earth. He has been brave enough to face and to feel the immensity of the loss. He has dared to share that with us and to hope we can wake up to save what's left of our world and our souls."

—JOANNA MACY, coauthor, *Active Hope: How to Face the Mess We're in Without Going Crazy*

Over the last decade or more we have become increasingly aware of how our materialistic, energy-intensive civilization has been destroying the fragile balance of the web of life that has sustained humanity and all living beings for millennia. Yet, while spiritual teachings tell us that the events in the outer world are a reflection of changes taking place in the inner worlds, we appear to have little awareness of how this outer darkening is reflected within.

This book, written between 2004 and the winter of 2012, tells the story of these inner changes that belong to our spiritual destiny and the fate of our planet. It is a witness to the darkening of the light of the sacred, reflected in our continued ecological destruction, and what this might mean to our shared destiny. With this darkening comes the danger that we may lose the opportunity for the global awakening that was possible at the beginning of the new millennium. This story of our collective destiny, however painful, needs to be heard if we are to take responsibility for the Earth and reclaim our sacred role as guardians of the planet.

176 PAGES ❧ PAPERBACK: $14.95, EBOOK: $9.99

FOR LOVE *of the* REAL
A Story of Life's Mystical Secret

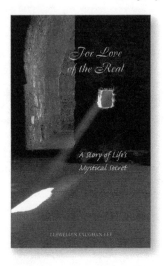

by Llewellyn Vaughan-Lee
with Hilary Hart

"Sufi scholars and practitioners I've met have often impressed me not only with their interest in knowing what is the self and the nature of reality, questions we Buddhists also struggle with, but also with their enthusiasm to understand how other traditions answer them. An exponent of the Naqshbandiyya-Mujaddidiyya Sufi Order, Llewellyn Vaughan-Lee's explanation in *For Love of the Real* of how to turn away from self-centeredness in the face of reality will appeal to readers who seek to lead a meaningful life."

—H.H. THE DALAI LAMA

At the root of every mystical calling is the search for what is Real. *For Love of the Real* follows this call, detailing the inner journey to Absolute Truth. Readers are guided through traditional experiences of the path—emptiness and the void, oneness, and communion with nature, for example. Particular direction is given for how contemporary seekers can—and must—engage with challenges unique to our times, such as extreme materialism and ecological devastation. *For Love of the Real* responds to the vital need for humanity to remember its own divine nature and restore mystical truth as the foundation of our inner and outer lives.

Based upon forty years of following the mystical path, Llewellyn Vaughan-Lee grounds this work in his own inner experiences and spiritual scripture. This is an intense evocation of the contribution that spiritual awareness can make, a clear and compelling call for humanity to return to the Real.

---

168 PAGES ❏ **HARDCOVER: $19.95**